Curious Cat's Way Out Bunch books feature
endangered and vulnerable living animals.
The information in each book is gathered
from known facts about them.

Research by Simon Greenaway.

With special thanks to Gray Jolliffe for all his help and encouragement.

© Green Arc Creations Ltd

First published by Green Arc Creations Ltd. 2011

All paper used comes from sustainably managed forests.

I'm Curious Cat on an adventure to see,
What the animal within these pages can be.
So let's read together and have a good look
And we shall find out by the end of this book.

Curious Cat is off to explore Greece.
'Help me choose the Greek flag,
and I will wear it on my hat.'

Ukraine

Peru

St. Vincent

Kenya

Brazil

USA

Japan

Switzerland

Greece

I can run on the waves with
Enormous webbed feet.
They help get me airborne
Where I spot things to eat.

My three metre wingspan makes flying a breeze,
As I soar over cliff tops and beaches and seas.

'I wonder what on earth this animal can be?
Do you think it can be one of these?'

Bream, roach and shrimp
And slippery eels,
Or mullet and dab
Are my favourite meals.

My feathers are tangled on top of my head,
They could do with a brushing it has to be said.

'Do you like eating apples, or ice cream?
Can you remember what this animal likes to eat?'

My eyes are pale green with the sharpest of sight,
They never stop searching for fish when in flight.

When stuffed full of fish
I've caught for my tea,
My bill is so huge
It's amazing to see.

'In Greece where this animal lives
there are many other creatures too.
I wonder if you have spotted some of them?'

European bee-eater

Common tree frog

Eel

Swallowtail Butterfly

Mediterranean
Spur-thigh tortoise

Rudd

Mullet

Large blue butterfly

Common pochard

Whether standing on sandbanks,
Or chattering in trees,
When night time approaches
I roost where I please.

With wings, bill and feathers one can only agree,
This must be a bird, but which one can it be?

Yes! A Dalmatian pelican, but spots I have none,
I'm a bird, not a dog, which is just as much fun.

Did you know.....

The Dalmatian pelican is one of the largest birds in the world, apart from emus and ostriches which are of course flightless.

The Dalmatian pelican has a wing span of up to 3.2 metres.

They have grey legs and feet with short webbed toes.

They have been heard to bark, hiss or grunt at times.

Dalmatian pelicans do most of their foraging and feeding at dawn and late afternoon.

They move their large bills in a side to side sweeping motion in shallow water, searching for food including fish, worms, shrimps and prawns. Beneath the bill is an orange pouch which is particularly vivid during the breeding season.

They choose islands or other inaccessible areas to breed within reed beds or in the open. There they build large loose nests of vegetation and twigs held together with mud and droppings.

Generally between two and four eggs are laid and take around thirty days to hatch.

When nesting they are easily panicked if approached and will crush their eggs or young as they flee. Once disturbed they will often leave eggs unattended and nestlings to starve.

The Dalmatian pelican is now the rarest of the seven species of pelican that exist today around the world.

They are threatened by drainage of their wetland habitat, mostly for agriculture, and persecuted by fishermen for the perceived competition to fish stocks.

In their Mongolian breeding grounds they are particularly at risk due to hunting by tribesmen for their bills which are used as traditional dagger sheathes.

If you would like to find out more information on endangered animals and how to help them, visit these websites:

WWF-UK - www.wwf.org.uk
The Edge programme - www.edgeofexistence.org
ARKive, images of life on Earth - www.arkive.org
Photograph: NHPA/Photoshot - www.nhpa.co.uk